CYBER DETECTIVES

A Fun Guide to Staying Safe Online

Vanya Gupta

ISBN 979-8-89744-020-7

Contents

Introduction to Cybersecurity

Imagine you're having the time of your life at a giant theme park, filled with exciting rides, fun games, and tasty treats. But just like in a real theme park, where you need to follow safety rules—like staying in your seat on a roller coaster, keeping an eye on your belongings, and not talking to strangers—you also need to stay safe when exploring the internet!

Cybersecurity is like having a superhero shield that protects you while you enjoy the online world. It helps keep you safe from things like tricky people, mean messages, or websites that might not be what they seem. Just as you wouldn't share your ticket with a stranger, you should never share personal information like your password or home address online.

It's also important to learn good online habits, like asking a trusted adult for help when something doesn't seem right—just like you would if you got lost in a theme park.

So, cybersecurity is really just a fancy word for making sure you have fun on the internet while staying safe—just like you would in your favorite theme park!

Fun Fact  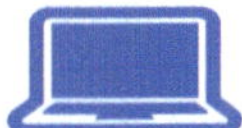

1. A "Hacker" Doesn't Always Mean a Bad Guy !

Some hackers are called "white-hat hackers", and they help keep the internet safe by finding and fixing problems. They're like cyber superheroes !

2. Passwords Love to Be Unique!

"THEY WERE WAY AHEAD OF US IN PASSWORDS."

Did you know the most common password in the world is 123456 ? □ That's like using the same key for every house! A strong password is like a secret code only you know.

3. Cyber Viruses Are Like Tiny Sneaky Robots!

A computer virus isn't a real bug, but it acts like one. It can spread from one computer to another, just like a sneeze spreads germs. That's why antivirus software is like medicine for your computer!

4. You Can Be a Cyber Detective!

Spotting fake websites or emails is like solving a mystery! If someone asks for your password or personal info online, you can say, "That's suspicious!" and report it.

5. The First "Computer Worm" Was a Joke!

The first computer worm, called the Morris Worm , was created in 1988. It wasn't supposed to cause harm but ended up slowing down the entire internet (which was very small back then)!

Online Behavior

Online behavior is how you act when you're using the internet, like when you're chatting with friends, playing games, or even posting on social media. Just like how we should be polite and kind to people when we talk to them, we should do the same when we're online. It's important to remember that the internet is like a big community, and everyone should treat each other with respect.

Risks of the Internet

1. Be Kind and Respectful

When you're online, treat others how you'd like to be treated. Just because you're behind a screen doesn't mean you can be rude, mean, or hurtful. If you wouldn't say something to someone in person, you shouldn't say it online either.

Example : If you see someone post something funny or cool, leave them a nice comment! If you see something you don't agree with, it's okay to share your thoughts, but always do it kindly.

2. Think Before You Post

Once something is posted online, it can be hard to take back. Always think, "Would I want everyone to see this? Is this something I'd be proud of forever?" Even if you delete a post, someone might have seen it already or even saved it.

Example: If you post a photo or comment, ask yourself if it's something that represents the best version of you. If not, it's better to keep it private.

3. Be Careful with Personal Information

Your personal information (like your full name, address, phone number, or school) is private and should be kept that way. Don't share these details online, and make sure you only share what's necessary.

Example: When you're playing a game or chatting online, don't tell strangers things like where you live or what school you go to. Just like you wouldn't tell a stranger on the street these things, don't do it online either.

4. Respect Other People's Privacy

Just like you don't want strangers looking through your personal things, it's important not to invade someone else's privacy. If someone doesn't want to share something or doesn't want their picture posted, respect their choice.

Example: If you're taking a group picture with your friends, ask them if they're okay with the picture being posted online first. If they say no, don't post it

5. Cyberbullying is Never Okay

Cyberbullying is when someone uses the internet to hurt or upset others on purpose. It can be sending mean messages, spreading rumors, or leaving hurtful comments. If you see it happening, speak up or tell an adult. It's important to stop bullying and support the person being hurt.

Example: If you see a friend being picked on in an online chat or game, Everything you do online creates a digital footprint—your online reputation. Keep it positive by posting, commenting, and sharing responsibly.

Example: If you make a fun video or share something cool, make sure it reflects the real you—a good friend, a good student, and someone others can trust.

6. Don't Talk to Strangers

Don't talk to strangers online. Only chat with people you know or on trusted platforms with parental supervision. If unsure, ask an adult.

Example: If you get a message from someone you don't know, tell an adult right away. They can help you figure out if it's safe.

7. Be Honest

If you make a mistake online, be honest about it and fix it. If you accidentally share too much information or post something that wasn't kind, don't be afraid to apologize and make it right.

Example: If you said something that hurt someone's feelings, apologize and explain that you didn't mean to. Everyone makes mistakes, but being honest helps you learn and grow.

Protecting Your Privacy

Online Security Quiz

Read each scenario and circle the option you would choose :

1. Your friends have started using a new social media app. The app requires the users to be 18 years or older.
   a. Lie about age and sign up.
   b. Get your friends to make a fake account.
   c. Don't agree to use the app

2. You get an email that you have won a cash prize. The mail suggests you to click on the attachment to claim the prize.
   a. Reply to the mail for more details
   b. Ignore the email and delete it immediately.
   c. Open the attachment

Create a Comic Strip

Draw your own comic strip about protecting your privacy. Use characters to show how to keep your information secure online. Refer the sample comic strip shown

Example:

Mrs. Know-It-All's Costly Click

Mrs. Know-It-All was a woman who believed she knew everything. She could name the capitals of every country, answer any tricky math problem, and even tell you how to train your pet hamster to juggle. But there was one thing she didn't know—how to spot a phishing scam.

One sunny morning, Mrs. Know-It-All sat at her desk, sipping tea, when she received an email with the subject, "URGENT: Your bank account has been compromised! Click here to secure your funds." The email looked so official, with fancy logos and everything.

"Ha! A scam? Not for me!" she said, rolling her eyes. "I'm a master at spotting scams."

But just to be safe, she clicked the link. A pop-up appeared, asking for her bank details. "Well, I do need to secure my account," she reasoned, typing in her username, password, and even her mother's maiden name (just in case).

Two days later, Mrs. Know-It-All checked her bank account. Her heart dropped. It was empty! "What in the world?!" she gasped, staring at the screen. Someone had taken all her money!

Panicked, she ran to her neighbor, Mr. Clueless, who always asked her for advice on everything. "I got scammed!" she cried.

Mr. Clueless scratched his head. "Did you click on any strange links recently?"

"Well... yes," Mrs. Know-It-All admitted, now feeling very embarrassed. "But it looked so real!"

"I think you just fell for a phishing scam," Mr. Clueless said, trying to sound smart.

"Phishing? I thought that was something you do with a fishing pole!" Mrs. Know-It-All exclaimed.

"No, no," Mr. Clueless said, "Phishing is when someone tricks you into giving away your personal info online."

Mrs. Know-It-All's eyes widened. "So I just gave my bank details to a stranger?"

"Yup," Mr. Clueless said, "but now you know better."

Mrs. Know-It-All stared at him, still in shock. "So, what should I do now?"

"Well," Mr. Clueless said, "the first thing you need to do is call your bank immediately! Let them know you think you've been scammed, and they can help lock your account to stop anyone from taking more money."

"Right! And then?" Mrs. Know-It-All asked, taking notes.

"Next, report the scam to the authorities or the website where the email came from," Mr. Clueless said. "That way, they can warn other people too."

Mrs. Know-It-All wrote that down. "What about my password? Should I change it?"

"Definitely!" Mr. Clueless replied. "You should change your passwords for any accounts linked to the scam. And set up two-factor authentication to make things extra secure."

Mrs. Know-It-All nodded, now feeling a bit more in control. She rushed off to do exactly what Mr. Clueless had told her.

After everything was sorted, she realized just how much she'd learned. From that day on, whenever she got an email that seemed too good to be true, she didn't click on it right away. She double-checked the link, asked a trusted adult, and made sure the message was really from her bank.

Though she still liked to think she knew everything, she finally admitted there was one thing she didn't: how to avoid getting tricked online. But now, she was a little wiser and a lot safer.

And remember, kids: if you ever get caught in a phishing scam, don't panic! Call your bank, report it, change your passwords, and always be cautious with emails. Safety first!

Valuable Insights From Mr.Clueless :

- Be cautious with emails that create urgency
- Report the scam to authorities or the website it came from
- Use strong, unique passwords for different accounts.
- Always verify links before clicking—hover over them to check the actual URL.

Phishing Detection Game

Can you identify the phishing emails from the real ones? Play the phishing detection game to test your skills.

Subject: Your Amazon Order Confirmation From: support@amazon.com Message: Hello Customer, Thank you for your recent order with Amazon. Your order will be shipped in 3-5 business days. You can track your order by visiting the link below: Track your order If you have any questions or need further assistance, feel free to contact our support team. Best regards, Amazon Support Team	Subject: You've won $500,000! Claim now! From: prizewinner@scam.com Message: Congratulations! You've been selected to receive a grand prize of $500,000! This incredible prize is waiting for you, but you must act immediately! Click the link below to claim your prize: Claim my prize now! Hurry! You have only 24 hours to claim your winnings before it's too late! Best regards, Prize Claim Team

Rules: How to Play:

- **Read Aloud:** One player reads an email from the list.
- **Decide Quickly:** Players have 30 seconds to judge if it's "Real" or "Fake."
- **Write Answers**: Write "Real" or "Fake" and highlight reasons if needed.

- **Score Points:**
  - **Correct:** 1 point.
  - Spot a **red flag** in a fake email: +1 point.
  - **Wrong:** 0 points.
  - **Tally Scores:** Add up points at the end to see who wins!

Learn About Passwords From - Mr. Grumblebeard

Once upon a time, in the vast and unpredictable seas, there was a notorious

pirate named Captain Grumblebeard. He was not known for his cunning or strategy, but rather for his immense fortune. One of his prized possessions was a grand treasure chest filled to the brim with glittering gold coins and dazzling jewels.

The Simple Code

Captain Grumblebeard, in his careless nature, decided to protect his treasure with a code. However, his choice in codes was as simple as his love for rum. He settled on "1234", thinking it would be easy to remember amidst the chaos of his pirate life. With a hearty laugh, he locked his treasure chest, feeling satisfied with his decision.

The Thieves' Opportunity

Little did Captain Grumblebeard know, his simple code was no match for the cunning thieves lurking in the shadows. Word spread quickly among them about the pirate's laughable code. One moonless night, the thieves sneaked aboard Captain Grumblebeard's ship and, with little effort, opened the chest. To the pirate's horror, by morning, his treasure was gone, leaving only an empty chest and a lesson to be learned.

The Lesson Learned

Captain Grumblebeard, though devastated, was not a pirate who wallowed in self-pity. He realized that the security of his treasure was only as strong as the code that protected it. Determined to never let such a misfortune befall him again, he sought advice from the wisest sailors on the seas. They taught him the importance of a strong code, one that was complex and unpredictable.

Protect Your Digital Treasures

In the modern world, we may not have physical treasure chests, but we do have digital treasures that are just as valuable. From personal photos and emails to financial information and sensitive documents, these digital assets need protection.

Like Captain Grumblebeard, we must learn that a strong password is essential.

Tips for a Strong Password :

1. **Length and Complexity:** Use at least 12 characters, combining upper and lower case letters, numbers, and symbols.
2. **Avoid Common Words:** Steer clear of easily guessed words like "password" or "123456".
3. **Use Unique Passwords:** Avoid using the same password across multiple accounts.
4. **Update Regularly**: Change your passwords periodically to enhance security.

5. **Utilize Password Managers:** Consider using a password manager to generate and store complex passwords securely.

Just as Captain Grumblebeard learned to protect his gold, we must protect our digital treasures with strong, secure passwords.

So, set sail with confidence, knowing your digital assets are safe from the modern-day thieves of the cyber world.

Create Your Own Password

Change each password to make it stronger . One example is done for you !

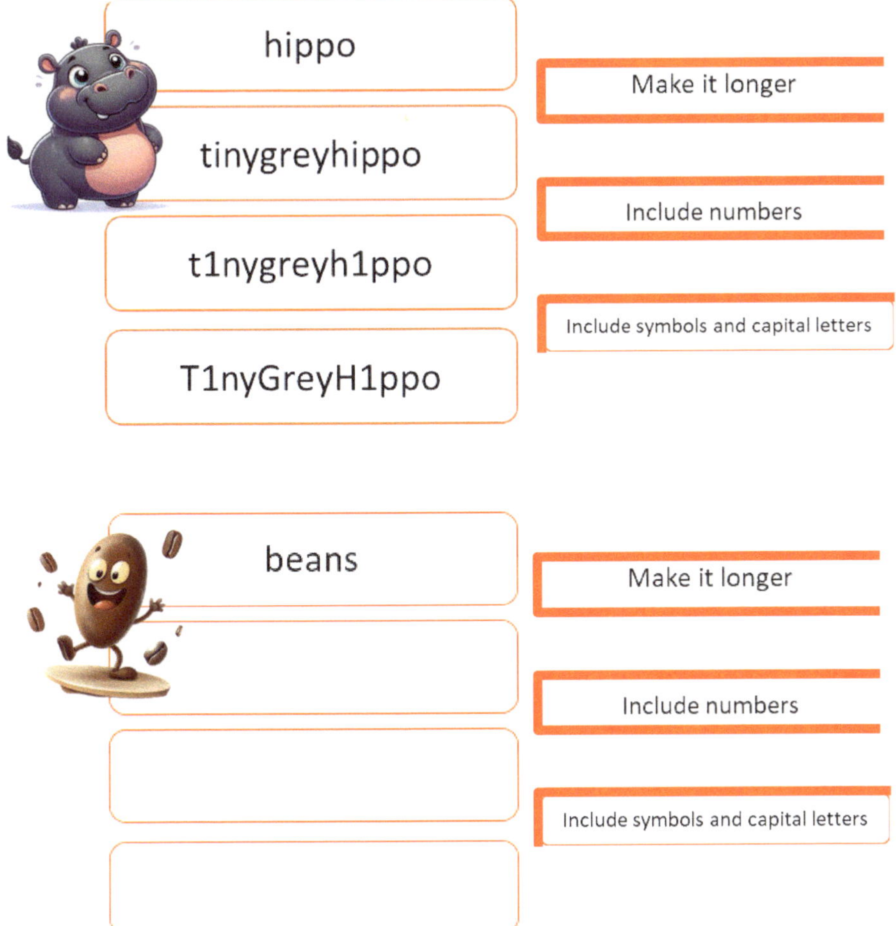

Digital Foot-Prints 

What Are Digital Footprints?

Imagine you are walking on the beach. Every step you take leaves a footprint in the sand. Similarly, when you do something online—like visiting a website, posting a photo, or sending a message—you leave **a digital footprint.**

This footprint is like a trail that shows what you've done on the internet. It can be:

Good footprints: Being kind online, learning new things, or creating helpful content.

Risky footprints: Sharing private information, visiting unsafe websites, or being unkind.

Just like footprints in the sand, digital footprints can be seen by others. So, it's important to leave footprints that are safe and positive!

How to Keep Your Digital Footprint Safe:

Think before you post: Always ask yourself, "Would I want everyone to see this?" if the answer is no, don't post it!

Use privacy settings: Make sure you know how to control who can see your posts on social media and who can access your personal information.

Protect your personal info: Never share sensitive information like your address, phone number, or passwords online.

Be respectful: If you're ever unsure about something you want to say or share, it's a good idea to take a moment and think about whether it's kind and respectful.

In the end, your digital footprint is like your online fingerprint—it's unique to you, and it can follow you around. So, making good choices online helps keep your digital footprint positive and safe!

Trail of Choices

Steps:

1. Each question is about a real-life online situation.
2. Choose A (Good Choice) or B (Risky Choice) for each scenario.
3. Draw a green footprint for good choices and a red footprint for risky ones.
4. Count your footprints at the end to see how safe your online trail is! Visual: Diagram of a path with green and red footprints.

Question 1: Strong Passwords
Scenario:
"You just got a new device. What do you do?"
•**A:** Set a strong password like "MyPet#123" (Green Footprint ).
•**B:** Use "1234" as your password (Red Footprint 👎).

Question 2: Sharing Personal Information
Scenario:
"You post a picture on social media. Someone comments, 'Nice picture! What's your phone number?'"
•**A:** Ignore the comment or block the person (Green Footprint 👍).
•**B:** Reply with your phone number (Red Footprint 👎).

Question 3: Clicking on Links
Scenario:
"You get a message from a stranger with a link that says 'Click here to win a prize!' What do you do?"
•**A:** Delete the message or report it as spam (Green Footprint 👍).
•**B:** Click the link immediately to see the prize (Red Footprint 👎).

Question 4: Downloading Free Apps
Scenario:
"You find a free game on a random website. What do you do?"
•**A:** Check if the website is safe and download only from trusted stores (Green Footprint).
•**B:** Download it right away without checking (Red Footprint ).

Question 5: Handling Mean Comments
Scenario:
"You see someone posting mean comments about your friend online. What do you do?"
•**A:** Support your friend and report the comment (Green Footprint ).
•**B:** Join in and post something mean too (Red Footprint).

My Digital Foot Prints !

Cyber Bullying

What is Cyberbullying?

Cyberbullying is when someone uses the internet, social media, or games to be mean, hurtful, or embarrassing to someone else. It can happen through messages, comments, posts, or even fake profiles. The tricky part is that it can happen anytime, anywhere, and sometimes the bully hides behind a fake name.

Examples of Cyberbullying

- Sending mean or threatening texts or DMs.
- Posting embarrassing photos or videos of someone without their permission.
- Spreading rumors or lies about someone online.
- Making fun of someone in a group chat or online game.
- Excluding someone from an online group or activity on purpose.

Why Cyberbullying is a Big Deal

- It can make people feel really sad, lonely, or even scared.
- Once something is posted online, it can spread fast and stay there forever.
- It can happen in front of a lot of people, making it even more embarrassing.

What to Do If You're Being Cyberbullied

1. Don't respond: Replying to a bully can make things worse.
2. Save the evidence: Take screenshots of the messages or posts.
3. Block the bully: Use the block button to stop them from contacting you.
4. Report it: Tell a trusted adult (like a parent or teacher) and report it to the app or website.
5. Talk to someone: Don't keep it to yourself—talk to a friend, family member, or counselor.

How to Be an Upstander, Not a Bystander

- If you see someone being cyberbullied, don't just watch—stand up for them!
- Report the bullying to an adult or the platform.
- Be kind and supportive to the person being bullied.

Gaming and Online Communities: Staying Safe and Having Fun

Online games and communities are awesome places to hang out, make friends, and have fun. But just like in real life, there are some risks. Here's how to stay safe while gaming and chatting online.

Risks to Watch Out For

1. Strangers: Not everyone online is who they say they are. Some people might pretend to be nice but have bad intentions.
2. Toxic behavior: Some players can be really mean, especially in competitive games.

3. Scams: Be careful of fake offers for free skins, coins, or cheats—they might be tricks to steal your info or hack your account.
4. Addiction: Spending too much time gaming can mess with your sleep, schoolwork, and mental health.

Stay Safe Online: Quick Tips

1. Protect Your Info: Use a unique username and never share personal details.
2. Chat Wisely: Avoid strangers, don't overshare, and block/report rude users.
3. Privacy First: Restrict messages to friends and turn off location sharing.
4. Spot Scams: Ignore sketchy links, downloads, and "too good to be true" offers.
5. Game Smart: Balance screen time with school, friends, and other activities.

Cyberbullying Awareness Challenge

Part 1: Spot the Cyberbullying

Read each scenario and decide if it is cyberbullying. Circle Yes or No, then explain your reasoning.

Scenario 1:

Sarah and her friends make fun of Emma's haircut in a group chat, sending mean messages like, "Your hair looks weird!" and "No one likes you anymore."

Is this cyberbullying? Yes / No

Why? ____________________

Scenario 2:

Jake shares a meme on social media. A classmate comments, "This is so dumb!" but deletes the comment after a few minutes.

Is this cyberbullying? Yes / No

Why? ____________________

Scenario 3:

Alex creates a fake profile to send mean messages to Ryan, calling him a "loser" and saying, "No one wants to be your friend."

Is this cyberbullying? Yes / No

Why? ____________________

Scenario 4:

Lily posts a picture of her dog on Instagram. A stranger comments, "Cute dog!"

Is this cyberbullying? Yes / No

Why? ____________________

Part 2: What Would You Do?

Scenario 5:

During an online game, another player repeatedly calls you names like "noob" and "loser" when you lose.

Is this cyberbullying? Yes / No

What would you do?

A. Ignore them and keep playing.

B. Call them names back.

C. Block and report them.

D. Tell a parent or teacher.

Part 3: Be an Upstander!

◆ Activity 1: Role-Playing

With a partner, act out how you would support a friend who is being bullied online. How can you help stop the bullying?

____

____

____

____

____

____

◆ Activity 2: Create a Poster

Design a poster to promote kindness online. Include: A catchy slogan (e.g., "Think Before You Type!").

Tips for staying safe.

A reminder to report cyberbullying.

Part 4: Reflection

Why is it important to stop cyberbullying?

What should you do if you or someone you know is being cyberbullied?

How can you make the internet a better place?

Cyber Detective Quiz

Are you ready to become a Cyber Detective?

1. You just got a new device. What is the best password to set?

   A. 1234 B. MyPet#123 C. password D. 1111

2. You post a picture online, and someone asks for your phone number. What should you do?

   A. Share your phone number with them.

   B. Ignore or block the person.

   C. Ask them for their number instead.

   D. Tell them you'll think about it.

3. You receive a message saying, "Click here to win a prize!" What's the safest action to take?

   A. Click the link immediately.

   B. Share the link with your friends.

   C. Delete the message and report it as spam.

   D. Save the link for later.

4. You find a free game on an unfamiliar website. What's the right thing to do?

   A. Download the game immediately.

   B. Check if the website is safe first.

   C. Share the game link with your friends.

   D. Download it and install antivirus later.

5. You see someone posting mean comments about your friend online. What should you do?

   A. Post something mean back to defend your friend.

   B. Ignore the comment and do nothing.

   C. Report the comment and support your friend.

   D. Share the mean comment with others.

---

1. B
2. B
3. C
4. B
5. C

YOU HAVE NOW UNLOCKED THE
CYBER DETECTIVE SKILLS

www.ingramcontent.com/pod-product-compliance
Lightning Source LLC
LaVergne TN
LVHW021347160826
845679LV00008B/1519